CRACKING THE LEGACY CODE

How To Pass Down Generational Wealth

TABLE OF CONTENTS

Chapter One
Steps to Building Generational Wealth Gods Way!

Here are the Steps to Building Generational Legacy

When you hear the words, *family legacy* you may think of the distribution of tangible assets, trusts and maybe even estate planning. While these factors are a part of **family legacy**, the largest bequest family members receive are the *non-material* gifts including:

- Attitudes
- Behaviors
- Beliefs
- Communication Styles
- Traditions
- Patterns
- Coping Mechanisms

These are the aspects of familial legacy that are often overlooked but remain so crucial to your present and your future.

Why? Because if there's anything that you've taken on that isn't serving you – it's important to observe it, understand it, and heal it.

Proverbs 13:22 NIV—A good person leaves an inheritance for their children's children, but a sinner's wealth is stored up the righteous.

Your thoughts and beliefs create your reality. However, just because you grew up with a certain set of beliefs, it doesn't mean that you have to keep them. You have the power to change the trajectory of your life and impact future generations.

So much of family legacy is passed on unintentionally by parents simply doing the best they can with what they know while attempting to, in parallel, process their own past. Legacy is then extended to children who live according to what they witness so much more than to what is told to them by their well-meaning parents.

Proverbs 13:22 Message—A good life get passed on to the grandchildren; ill-gotten wealth ends up with good people.

The best definition for legacy is a spiritual, physical, or tangible financial gift passed on to someone else of the world at large.

It means something transmitted by a person to another person for continued legacy.

It's recorded in Biblical History that the Apostle Timothy received the transfer of his mother and grandmother's anointing.

2 Timothy 1:5-7 Message—That precious memory triggers another: your honest faith-and what a rich faith it is, handed down from your grandmother Lois to your mother Eunice, and to you! And the Special gift of ministry you received when I laid hands on you and prayed—keep that ablaze! God doesn't want us to be shy with His gifts but bold and loving and sensible.

NOTES

CHAPTER TWO

KEY STEPS REQUIRED TO BUILD WEALTH

Step 1 - Understand your God authorized purpose.

Step 2 - Ask God to give you clear vision for creating your legacy!

A God vision prevents a believer from being full of self, and conscious of God's purpose for why He placed us here.

Habakkuk 2: 2-3—Message Bible—And then God answered: Write this. Write what you see. Write it out in big letters so that it can be read on the run. This vision-message is a witness pointing to what's coming. It aches for the coming– it can hardly wait! And it doesn't lie. It seems slow in coming, wait. It's on its way. It will come right on time.

God's not going to waste visions and opportunities on you if you are not willing to ask for help and take the faith risk.

A. Ask for help
B. Write the vision or plan down for your immediate family in order for generations to come to understand what your family legacy or dynasty is.
C. Figure out what is required for you to build your legacy.

Step 3 - Ask yourself real questions like; what tools do I need, or what education is required for me to create generational wealth and legacy.

- Do I really know God's purpose for my life? Your why?
- Do I need to work on my talent for skillset?

Daniel 1:5 " the king appointed for them a daily ration from the king's choice food and from the wine which he drank, and appointed that they should be educated three years, at the end of which they were to enter the king's personal service."

- Do I understand how money works?
- Do I need more Financial Literacy education—Will, Trust and Investments?
- How do I become a first-time home buyer?
- How to start my own business?
- What do I need to learn about setting my kids up at an early age with educational IUL.?
- How do I become a first-time home buyer?

Step 4 - Start Planning

Building wealth starts with making a financial plan. That means taking the time to identify your goals and game out how you can accomplish them.

Plenty of people dread the "b" word, but budgeting is a key plank in your wealth building strategy. Building a budget and sticking to it helps increase your chances of carrying out your plan and achieving your financial goals.

Budgets also help you understand where your money goes each month and prevent behaviors that can endanger your goals, like overspending.

NOTES

_____

_____

_____

_____

_____

_____

_____

_____

_____

_____

_____

_____

_____

_____

_____

_____

_____

_____

_____

_____

_____

_____

_____

_____

Chapter Three

USE YOUR IMAGINATION FOR MAKING A DIFFERENCE

Vision vs. Purpose

Vision builds on purpose, but there are differences between the two:

- Purpose clarifies; vision motivates.
- Purpose is the reason you live; vision is the song your heart sings.
- Purpose gives meaning; vision prompts action.
- Purpose uses your own words to capture God's common purposes for all disciples; vision evokes awe and releases imagination.

Romans 8:28 ESV—And we know that for those who love God all things work together for good, for those who are called according to his purpose.

Your Faith Vision is a picture of God's preferred future.

Pictures have power because of the way they focus us. The picture needs to be clear and it must capture what God wants to create through you and be focused on the outcome rather than the process.

Every Individual, Husband, Wife or Leader should know:

1. What is the role of wealth in our lives?

2. What do I hope the inheritance is going to do in my child's life? Are my children clear on the vision and what is required of them?

3. How do I create inheritances that will further our family Christian values?

Test your Legacy Vision with these Questions:

- Does it have God's DNA?

- Can I visualize what God's purpose is? Is it clear?

- Does it focus on the "how to" for an expected end?

- Does it engage my passion and purpose and benefit others?

- Do I have everything needed to achieve it?

Action Step. Translate God's vision for legacy into faith goals and practical steps.

Hebrew 11:1 – Now faith is being sure of what we hope for and certain of what we do not see.

Don't you realize that in a race everyone runs, but only one person gets the prize? So run to win! All athletes are disciplined in their training. They do it to win a prize that will fade away, but we do it for an eternal prize. So I run with purpose in every step. I am not just shadowboxing. I discipline my body like an athlete, training it to do what it should. Otherwise, I fear that after preaching to others I myself might be disqualified.

I Corinthians 9:24-27

Next Action Step – Integrate your family or loved ones into the plan by making it clear what their role will be and the steps to continuing generational legacy for 100 years.

Amos 3:3 – Can two walk together, unless they are agreed?

NOTES

Chapter Four

INVEST IN YOUR FAMILY

Spend some time this year on home improvement; purpose to work on your agreement, faith, words spoken and seed required to grow your family.

You will never look back on life and think, "I spent too much time with my kids or spouse."

No one is useless in this world who lightens the burdens of another!

Charles Dickens

Make people greater than yourself and you will live forever.

Leaving behind a legacy means making an impact that will last long after you die. It could be financial, with something you create, or through the people you touch while you're alive. The good news is, it's never too late to start working on building a legacy that will outlive you.

7 Ways to Start Building Powerful Legacy:

1. Start with those closest to you like a family member or friend! Or the ones you spend the most time with like in the household of faith.

2. Build a circle of trust, honor, and value. Be open and vulnerable with each other. Ask God to give you grace for everyone!

3. Find your family purpose and identify everyone's gift or skillset.

4. Do what matters now. Everyone who's at the end of life says it goes by fast.

5. Become the Best You in Your Family, Church Partnership! Everyone has at least two selves. Bring out the best one.

6. Write the vision down and make it clear on what's expected of them in order to receive the inheritance.

7. Elevate the needs of others over your own and think generational.

"No one is useless in this world who lightens the burdens of another."

Charles Dickens

Wisdom Nugget:

If you plan on leaving generational wealth with family, make sure you sit down with your children with a financial educator to make sure they are financially literate when it comes to money and how to handle your business affair (trust) before you depart!

You can help your kids create a path to support themselves by teaching them about personal finance. Giving your kids a financial education is one of the most important things you can do to start building generational wealth. It starts with having open conversations about money at home so your kids know they can ask questions.

Leaving behind a legacy means making an impact that will last long after you die. It could be financial, with something you create, or through the people you touch while you're alive. The good news is, it's never too late to start working on building a legacy that will outlive you.

Jesus said, it was imperative (better for the disciples, You and me) that I go away! Why? Because He needed to pass on Kingdom Legacy for us to advance the Kingdom of God!

All families have a set of beliefs, values, and attitudes that are passed down from generation to generation through the messages that children receive from their parents.

NOTES

Chapter Five

LEGACY MUST BECOME A MINDSET

Before It Can Become, a Reality!

Ask yourself this question, what message will our children carry to their children? If single, what message or imprint are you making those around you or someone else's kids? Fathers' what impression are we intentionally making on our wives, children, associates, church or our communities?

When we weigh what we want now against what we really want later, we realize how temporary satisfaction pales in comparison to a legacy built on purpose and generational fulfillment.

Deuteronomy 8:18 But remember the LORD your God, for it is he who gives you the ability to produce wealth, and so confirms his covenant, which he swore to your ancestors, as it is today.

Let's be clear. An inheritance is not limited to money. It also includes godly character and qualities like integrity and trustworthiness.

"The rich rule over the poor, and the borrower is slave to the lender."

Proverbs 22:7 (NIV)

Most Millionaires will not Leave an Inheritance to their children or anyone else that will squander their money, property, or family treasures.

Jesus said, it was imperative (better for the disciples and you and me) that I go away. Why? Because He needed to pass on Kingdom Legacy for us to advance the Kingdom of God.

All families have a set of beliefs, values and attitudes that are passed down from generation to generation through the messages that children receive from their parents.

Legacy must become a mindset before it can become a reality!

What message will your children carry to their children? If single, what message or imprint are you making on those around you or someone else's kids?

- When we weigh what we want *now* against what we really want *later*, we realize how temporary satisfaction pales in comparison to a legacy built on purpose and generational fulfillment.

Deuteronomy 8:18 – But remember the Lord your God, for it is he who gives you the ability to produce wealth, and so confirms his covenant, which he swore to your ancestors, as it is today.

Financial Wisdom Nugget:

Whole life policies are the least risky type of permanent life insurance. Their guarantees facilitate growth of generational wealth because a policyholder knows just how much their policy will earn in a given year, with non-guaranteed dividends as an added bonus. A tax-free death benefit is guaranteed as well.

Let's be clear, an inheritance is not limited to money. It also includes Godly character and qualities like integrity and trustworthiness.

Proverbs 2:7 – The rich rule over the poor, and the borrower is slave to the lender.

Most millionaires will not leave an inheritance to their children or anyone else that will squander their money, property, or family treasures.

How Do We Create Legacy?

What's the Template?

God wants us to be able to hear from Him and to serve people in His name . . . not to be in bondage to payments or live financially defeated lives. He want us to have freedom and options.

- Many of us sense God calling us to do great things for Him, but when we're in debt, we can't.
- Many of us dream of doing great things in life but we don't.
- If we change our mindset, we change our future.

NOTES

CHAPTER 6

HEALTHY FAMILIES = HEALTHY COMMUNITIES

Wisdom Nugget:

Legacy is About Wealth Transfer

Abraham is best known for the depth of his faith in God and being the father of many nations. In Apostle Paul's letter to the Christians in Rome, speaking by the prompting of the Holy Spirit, he reveals in:

Romans 8:17 that," And if children, Then Heirs; Heirs of God, and Joint – Heirs with Christ."

Speaking further on this, Paul writes thus to the church in Ephesus:

Ephesians 3:6 – that the Gentiles should be fellow heirs, and of the same body and partakers of His promise in Christ by the gospel.

Clearly, Paul drives the same point home; as a Christian, you are an heir of the promise. But what exactly does it mean to be an heir of the promise?

To be an heir of God and a co-heir with Christ means that just like Abraham you have been made a partaker of the promise of God in Christ, which has qualified you for adoption into God's family and a rightful and authoritative owner of everything that belongs to God.

Galatians 4:6-7 Living Bible – And because we are his sons God has sent the Spirit of his Son into our hearts, so now we can rightly speak of God as our dear Father. Now we are no longer slaves, but God's own sons. . .

Important Insight

1. It means that everything God has belongs to you.

So, just like Abraham, who was known as . . ." *possessor of heaven and earth;"*

Genesis 4:19 – In Christ, you have equally been made possessor of heaven and earth.

2. Again, Paul leaves with an undeniable truth on this when he says: Ephesians 1:3 "Blessed be the God and Father of our Lord Jesus Christ, who hath blessed us with all spiritual blessings in heavenly places in Christ."

As an heir of God and a co-heir with Christ, your blessing isn't a promise, rather it's a reality; it has been done already.

3. The blessing is simply legacy that God chose to leave His children as an inheritance.

Financial Wisdom Nugget:

Generational wealth includes financial assets — such as property, investments, money, or anything with a monetary value — that you pass down from one generation to the next. Intangibles like financial education, values, and habits are an equally important part of the equation.

NOTES

Chapter Seven

How to Pass Down Generational Wealth

A critical step in building generational wealth is to create an estate plan which will ensure that in the event of death or incapacitation, your assets would be divided according to your wishes.

There are several steps that one can take to pass down generational wealth.

Here are a few and at the end of the book you will see a special bar code or email for free consultation.

1. Write a Will

A will should provide specific instructions on your last wishes and assets. Understanding the requirements in your state is very important to ensure that your will is enforceable. Also, when you have young children, a will helps communicate your wishes regarding their care. You can also list your financial assets to make it easier for your family members to locate them. When you don't have a will, you leave the decision up to the state when it comes to your children, property, and assets.

2. Set- Up a Trust

A trust, commonly referred to as a trust fund, is a legal entity you can use to hold and transfer assets to your beneficiaries. It is another option to consider for parents of minor children. Trusts can be expensive, but they also provide other benefits such as avoiding or reducing estate and gift taxes depending on the size of your estate.

3. Name Account Beneficiaries

To ensure that your assets pass down to the beneficiaries of your choice, it is sometimes as easy as naming specific beneficiaries for each account. Naming beneficiaries can save your loved ones a lot of time and energy in the event of your death, especially if they are adults.

Proper estate planning is an essential part of passing down generational wealth. Therefore, it's important to consult with an estate attorney to ensure that you have a solid estate plan.

Take Advantage of Life Insurance

Life insurance is a great tool to pass down wealth. It provides a safety net for your family if you were to die unexpectedly. If you have children or dependents who rely on your income, their financial situation would be negatively impacted by an eventual passing.

Financial Wisdom Nugget:

Why and how do millionaires use life insurance?

For many rich people, it makes sense to purchase whole life insurance, because this kind of policy can provide a death benefit to loved ones that is generally tax free. And this money can be used to pay estate or inheritance taxes, so that other estate assets do not have to be liquidated to cover this cost

Generational Wealth Building Principles

In 2019 CNBC's headline blared, "Here's how to prepare your heirs for the $68 trillion 'Great Wealth Transfer'." This "Advisor Insight" featured hot off the press research by Cerulli Associates, a major wealth management firm. The article's key point:

Baby Boomers are set to pass to their children a mind-boggling $68 trillion – the biggest generational wealth transfer ever!

The report echoes the words of many other international financial analysts who point increasingly to the impending and momentous tidal wave of cash and assets taking place *right now*.

$68 trillion? Who can even comprehend that much money? But what does that mean to you and me? What can it mean for the Kingdom? Saudi Arabia's royal family $1.4 trillion.

The wealthiest royal family in the world is the House of Saud, which is estimated to be worth more than a jaw dropping $1.4 trillion.

Financial Wisdom Nugget:

A Wealth Maximization Account combines dividend-paying whole life insurance with a type of supplemental insurance called a paid-up additions rider (PUAR). Adding a PUAR to your whole life policy allows you to "overfund" it in the first several years of ownership. In fact, in as few as 7 years, a Wealth Maximization Account may earn enough in guaranteed cash value and non-guaranteed dividend payments that they cover the cost of premiums. PUARs can also be structured so that the policy is "paid-up" by the time you retire. And if you already own a variable or universal policy, you can structure a 1035 Exchange, where cash value in your existing policy is used to purchase a PUAR in one lump sum.

If you have a serious goal to grow generational wealth, dividend-paying whole life insurance with a PUAR is proven to be the fastest and safest financial tool to help you do it.

Know this . . . supernatural sudden wealth transfers have already happened. Six are mentioned in Scripture: Abraham (Genesis 12:10), Isaac 26:1), Jacob (Genesis 31), Joseph (Genesis 41), Israel (Exodus 3:19-22), and Solomon (I Kings 10:23).

Prosperity, possessing the land, and expanding your borders is not man's idea. It is from God Almighty, and it's for you today.

Jesus, Himself, promised that those who have sacrificed anything, including houses and lands, for His sake and the Gospel's will "receive a hundredfold now in this time – houses . . . and lands . . . and in the age to come, eternal life" (Mark 10:29-30 NKJV).

Numerous stories and sayings from the Bible, written thousands of years ago, illustrate basic financial concepts that are as relevant as ever in the modern world.

NOTES

CHAPTER EIGHT

TAKE BIG ACTION STEPS

1. Set Priorities

Proverbs 24:27 – *Put your outdoor work in order and get your fields ready; after that, build your house.*

So in modern terms, this proverb means that you need to set priorities with your money. Make sure you save enough to cover the essentials – whatever you need to keep yourself alive and able to work – before spending money on creature comforts. In other words, set aside money to pay all the bills before you spend any on new clothes.

2. Make a Budget

Luke 14:28-30 – *Suppose one of you wants to build a tower. Won't you first sit down and estimate the cost to see if you have enough money to complete it? For if you lay the foundation and are not able to finish it, everyone who sees it will ridicule you, saying, "This person began to build and wasn't able to finish."*

This Biblical saying is about budgeting. You know you need to cover the cost of necessities first – but those costs don't always come up right away, so you need to plan for them or make a budget. Some major expenses, such as rent payments, only come due once per month. Others, like home insurance premiums, only come due once annually. Planning ahead and saving for those intermittent (but known) expenses is a key component of budgeting.

For example, suppose you earn $600 weekly. Out of that, you spend $50 on groceries, $10 on gas for your car, and $40 to pay the monthly electric bill, which happens to be due this week. At this point, you might think you've covered all your essential expenses, and the remaining $500 is free to spend as you like. However, if you just blow through that "extra" $500 every week, you'll be in for a rude awakening when your $700 rent is due at the end of the month.

3. Build an Emergency Fund

The average American family is just one to two paychecks away from being homeless. Genesis 41:34-36 — Let Pharaoh appoint commissioners over the land to take a fifth of the harvest of Egypt during the seven years of abundance. They should collect all the food of these good years that are coming and store up the grain under the authority of Pharaoh, to be kept in the cities for food. This food should be held in reserve for the country, to be used during the seven years of famine that will come upon Egypt, so that the country may not be ruined by the famine.

In this passage from Genesis, Joseph interprets a dream the Pharaoh has had about seven fat cows grazing by a river that get swallowed up by seven skinny cows. Joseph concludes that the seven fat cows in the dream represent seven years of prosperity for Egypt, which will be followed by seven years of famine. To plan ahead for this disaster, Joseph advises the Pharaoh to store up grain during the seven good years and use that stored grain to get the country through the seven hard years to follow.

No matter whether you believe Joseph had a divine gift for interpreting dreams, there's no denying that the advice he gives the Pharaoh is fundamentally sound. It always makes sense to save resources in good times so you have them to help you get through lean times. In modern-day America, "lean" years are less likely to be a literal famine than some sort of financial crisis, such as a job loss or a health problem that saddles you with hefty medical bills. Regardless, Joseph's basic strategy – setting aside money for future emergencies – still holds true.

Instead of storing up cash for seven years, they say you should set aside roughly six months' worth of living expenses in an emergency fund (more if you're self-employed or have a fluctuating income). And since you can't predict exactly when a financial crisis will hit the way Joseph could, this money should be kept in cash or safe investments that should hold their value, so your money is there to draw on whenever you happen to need it.

Financial Wisdom Nugget:

Permanent life insurance plans enable policyholders to accumulate cash value in addition to the death benefit. They can use these funds to pay their premiums, take out a loan at a lower rate than banks offer, and supplement their retirement income. Additionally, according to Investopedia, insureds can utilize the cash value built-up in their policies to "create an investment portfolio that maintains and accumulates wealth."

4. Avoid Debt

> *Proverbs 22:7* – The rich rule over the poor, and the borrower
> is *slave* to the lender.

This proverb takes no skill to interpret. It describes debt as a kind of slavery – and modern Americans appear to agree. A survey by the Pew Charitable Trusts found that for many Americans, debt is a condition that lasts a lifetime and is impossible to escape.

The survey found that 80% of all Americans are in debt, and a majority of the oldest Americans are still carrying some form of debt in retirement. And 70% of those surveyed said debt was a necessity in their lives – something they didn't want, but still couldn't imagine living without.

All that debt takes a toll on those who carry it, both mentally and physically.

A 2014 article in Health reports that high levels of debt are associated with anxiety, depression, and relationship problems. Debt can also be linked to high blood pressure, lowered immunity, and a host of physical symptoms, including headaches, back pain, and ulcers.

5. Diversify Your Investments

Ecclesiastes 11:2 – Invest in seven ventures, yes, in eight; you do not know what disaster may come upon the land.

This line from Ecclesiastes is a short, clear explanation of why it makes sense to diversify your investments. Nearly any type of investment can fall victim to "evil" of some sort, whether it's a plague of locusts that wipes out a grain crop, or a market crash that reduces the value of stocks or real estate. So it makes sense to put money into many different types of investments so that a single disaster can't cost you everything you have.

For instance, if you were a merchant in Biblical times, hoping to make money by trading cloth or spices with neighboring countries, it wouldn't make sense to load all your cargo onto a single ship. If that one ship sank, you'd lose everything you had in one blow. However, if you divided up your cargo among seven or eight ships, all headed along different routes, the chances that all of them would sink would be very low. So even if you lost one or two ships, you could still hope to earn enough from the others to make a profit.

It's a basic principle of investing that the more you diversify, the more you reduce your risk. Investing in 100 different stocks – for instance, by buying shares in an index fund – is far safer than investing in just a single stock.

6. Reduce Risk as You Age

Ecclesiastes 5:13-14 – I have seen a grievous evil under the sun: wealth hoarded to the harm of its owners, or wealth lost through some misfortune, so that when they have children there is nothing left for them to inherit.

In this story from Ecclesiastes, a father loses everything on a bad investment and has nothing to leave to his son. This is unfortunate for the son, but in the modern world, it could be a disaster for the father as well. That's because his bad business venture wouldn't just wipe out his son's inheritance – it could wipe out his own retirement savings as well.

People today live longer than ever before.

According to data from the National Institute on Aging, the average life expectancy in many developed countries is more than 80 years, and about 12% of the population is over 85 years of age. This number is expected to grow dramatically over the next few decades.

Because people are living longer, they're also spending more years in retirement. Today's 65-year-old retirees could easily need their retirement savings to last them 20 years or even longer. So if you speculate with your income when you're in your 60s, it's not just your kids' inheritance you're putting at risk – it's the money you need to live on for the next 10, 20, or even 30 years. If you lose a big chunk of your nest egg, you could end up having to put off your retirement because you don't have enough savings to support yourself.

If you want to be sure you have enough to retire on – and, ideally, something to leave to your kids when you're gone – you need to reduce your investment risk as you age. As you approach retirement age, you should gradually move your money out of high-risk investments, such as stocks, and into lower-risk investments like bonds and annuities that can give you a modest, steady income.

7. Make a Financial Plan

Proverbs 21:5 – The plans of the diligent lead to profit as surely as haste leads to poverty.

This final rule from Proverbs more or less sums up all the others. Budgeting, planning for retirement, saving for emergencies – they're all different ways of being diligent by planning ahead.

Making a financial plan is a three-step process:

Identify Your Goals. It's much easier to convince yourself to save and invest when you have a clear sense of what you're saving for. Depending on where you are in life, your financial goals could include paying off student loans, buying your first home, financing your kids' college education, or investing for retirement. Write down your personal goals, and go back to them from time to time to see if they've changed.

Evaluate Your Situation. Next, figure out what your current financial situation is. This is a step you can take on your own or with help from an accountant or financial advisor. Determine your current net worth, how much you're earning, how much you're spending, and what kind of return you're currently getting on your investments.

List Steps to Take.

Now that you know both where you are and where you want to go, all you have to do is figure out what steps you need to take to get from point A to point B. For instance, suppose your goal is to buy a house in five years and you think you need $55,000 for a down payment. If you already have $15,000 saved up, then you know you need to save another $40,000 over the next five years – an average of $8,000 per year. If you're currently saving only $5,000 every year, then you need to either make more money, spend less, or earn more on your investments – or all three – to hit your goal within five years. Alternatively, you could revise your goal, planning to buy a cheaper starter home that requires a smaller down payment of only $40,000 – a goal you can meet without making any changes.

Without a financial plan, it's easy to drift through life, earning and spending money with no real thought for the future. Writing out a financial plan and checking it every few months to see whether you're on track, helps ensure that you know what you want out of life and are on a path to get it.

NOTES

FINAL THOUGHTS:

As you get older, leaving a legacy may become increasingly important. It's comforting to know that after you're gone, a part of you will remain. Your family and friends will never forget you, but "legacy" goes beyond memories.

It's also important to consider your financial legacy, which refers to the assets you'll leave behind for your loved ones. As you get older, leaving a legacy may become increasingly important. It's comforting to know that after you're gone, a part of you will remain.

The overall message the Bible sends about money isn't that money itself is bad – it's just that it isn't the most important thing in life.

When used wisely – to support yourself, care for your family, and help those in need – (Community, Church etc.) money is a useful tool and should always have a mission.

However, you should control your money – you shouldn't let it control you. Rather than obsessing about how much money you have and how you can make more, take some time to be grateful for what you already have. That's a bit of Biblical wisdom that can benefit even the most experienced investor.

FOR COMPLIMENTARY CONSULTATION ON HOW TO CREATE LEGACY

SCAN THE BAR CODE BELOW OR EMAIL ME TODAY!

HEGEMON GROUP INTERNATIONAL

ANTHONY MCFARLAND
FINANCIAL EDUCATOR

 1-800-280-0628

 Dranthonymcfarland@gmail.com

FREE CONSULTATION

Licene # 4181747

Book Credits:

- Money Crashers' – Biblical financial tips
- Mila Araujo – the balance
- Daily Capital

(Special Expert for Book)

Dr. Anthony McFarland agrees with several other professional financial educators that as you get older, leaving a legacy may become increasingly important. It's important to know that after your gone, a part of you will remain. Building a family legacy gives you an opportunity to live for a purpose that's bigger than yourself. It allows you to change your family tree, not just for your children, but for generations to come! You can decide to use everything you have—wealth, resources, talent and relationships—to bless those around you.

Leaving behind a legacy means making an impact that will last long after you die. It could be financial, with something you create, or through the people you touch while you're alive. The good news is, it's never too late to start working on building a legacy that will outlive you.

IT'S YOUR CHOICE!